THE CHANGING FACES OF

BOOK TWO

Julie Kennedy

Published by
Robert Boyd Publications
260 Colwell Drive
Witney, Oxfordshire OX8 7LW

First published 1997

ISBN: 1 899536 23 X

OTHER TITLES IN THE

CHANGING FACES SERIES

Botley and North Hinksey
Bladon with Church Hanborough and Long Hanborough
Cowley: Book One
Cowley: Book Two
Cumnor and Appleton with Farmoor and Eaton
Eynsham: Book One
Headington: Book One
Headington: Book Two
Jericho: Book One
Littlemore and Sandford
Marston: Book One
Marston: Book Two
Summertown and Cutteslowe
St Ebbes and St Thomas: Book One
St Ebbes and St Thomas: Book Two
St Clements and East Oxford: Book One
Wolvercote with Wytham and Godstow
Woodstock: Book One

Forthcoming

Banbury
Cowley Works
Faringdon
Jericho: Book Two
Kennington
North Oxford
Oxford City Centre
Thame
Walton Manor
West Oxford
Witney

Printed and bound in Great Britain at The Alden Press, Oxford

Contents

Cover illustrations

Front: Tommy Robinson at work in his butchers shop.

Back: Looking up the hill towards Old Woodstock.

Acknowledgements

Thanks are due to the following for permission to use photographs in this publication: Nuala La Vertue at Oxfordshire Photographic Archives (OPA); Oxford and County newspapers; Chipping Norton Historical Society; Jeremys (Oxford Stamp Centre); Woodstock British Legion. Thanks also to Becky Vickers for the proof-reading.

For photographs and information on Woodstock, I would like to thank the following: Richard and John Banbury, Mr and Mrs Beckett, Sue Brooks, Misses J & S Clothier, Jane Dalton, Betty Danbury, David Dickinson, Eileen Cross, Pat Crutch, Agnes East, Pansy Fitchett, Ann Gardener, Rosemary Giraud, Ann Grant, D. Harrison, Mr and Mrs Jakeman, Michael Jordon, Mrs D. Lambourne, Mr and Mrs Margetts, Gerry and Cedric Moss, Mrs Neller, Sandra Scarsbrook, Cynthia Smith, Dulcie Smith, Mr and Mrs Symons, Peter Tothill, Audrey Turner, Bernice Osborne, Mrs Wastie, Marie Woolliscroft, Mr and Mrs B. Ward.

Preface

In response to the enjoyment so many people expressed in the first book on Woodstock published last year, and the realisation with hindsight they had photographs that could have been included, a second book has been prepared. More detailed text was included in Book One as, of course, there was originally only to be the one volume. Book Two is designed to be a companion to the first volume and I have tried to avoid giving the same information except where necessary. I trust that this will not inconvenience any readers too greatly.

Woodstock residents have a wealth of photographs and memorabilia in their possession and I feel privileged that they have been so willing to let me use these treasures. Although most of the original photographs are in good condition, some are over 100 years old. I hope that the interesting content of these earlier photographs will compensate for any reduction in clarity caused by their age.

I am aware that some errors occurred in the naming of individuals in Book One and doubtless there will be some errors in this new book, too. I would be pleased to hear from anyone who can correct these errors or supply names where they are missing. I would like to take this opportunity to place on record that the policeman in the photograph on page 14 in Book One is not Sergeant Jordon but rather another, as so far unidentified, policeman.

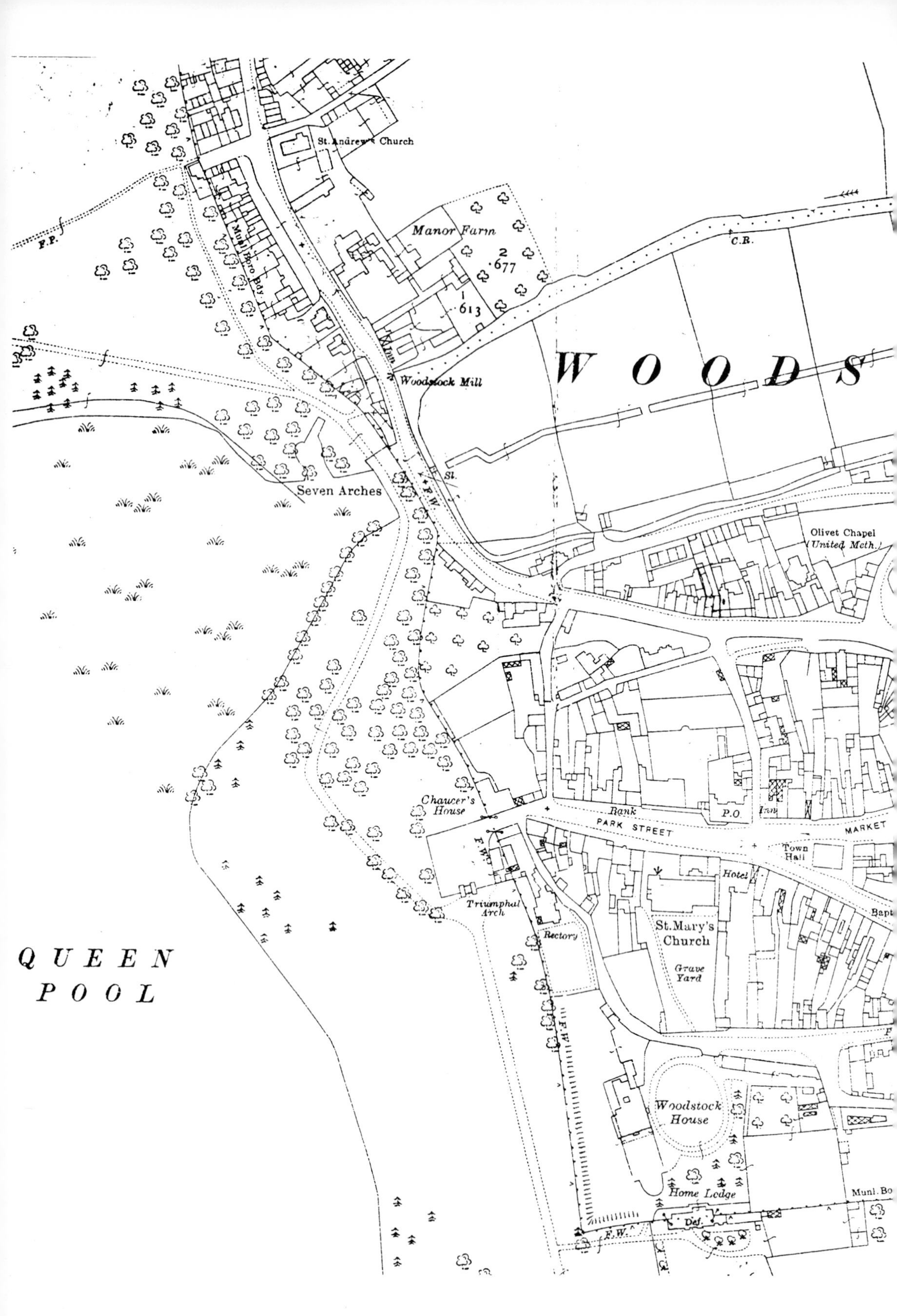

A 1922 Map of Woodstock

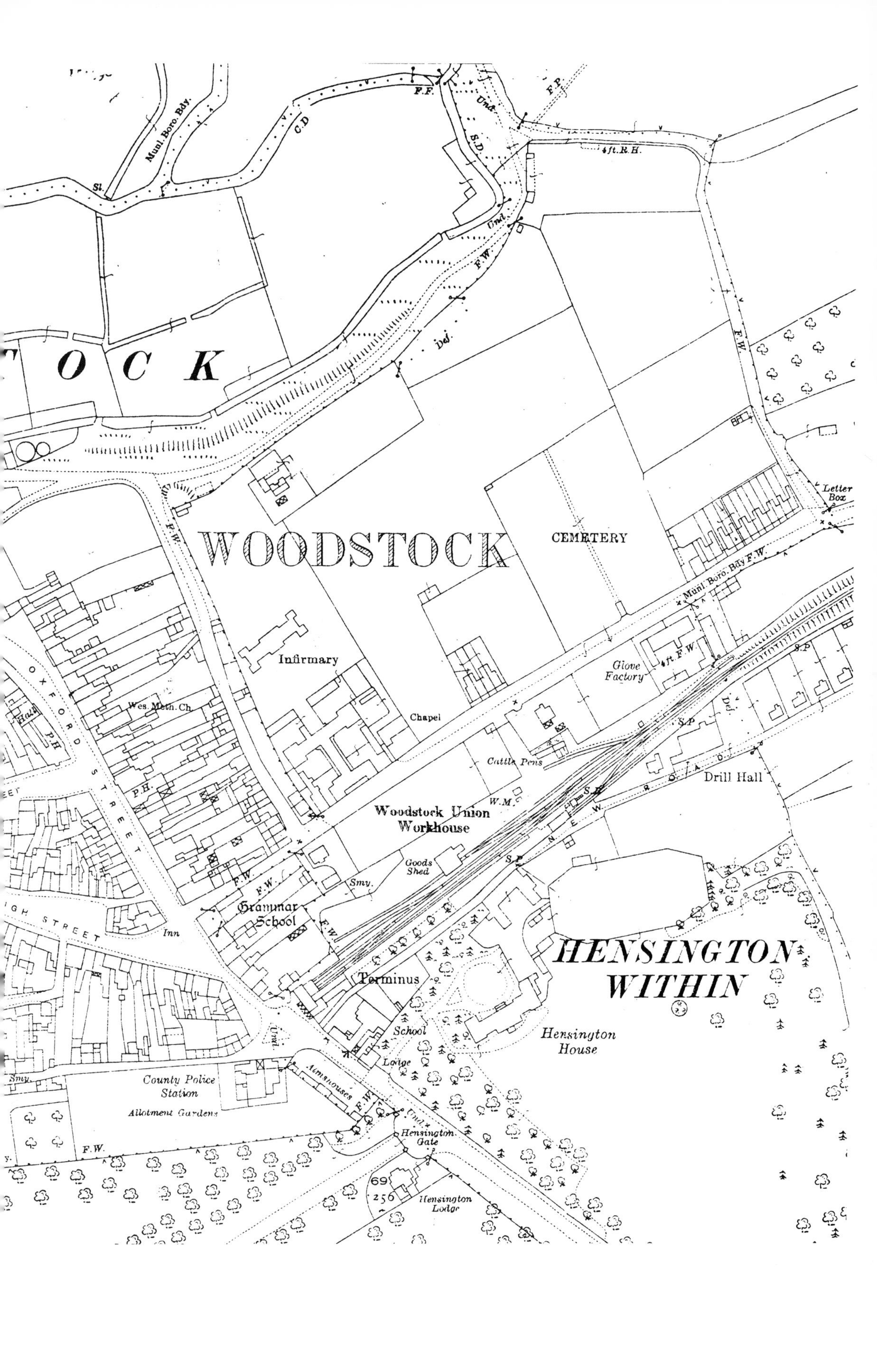

Munl. Boro. Bdy.
C.D
F.F.
Und.
S.D.
F.P.
4ft.R.H.
Und.
F.W.
Def.
F.W.
O C K
WOODSTOCK
CEMETERY
Letter Box
Munl. Boro. Bdy. F.W.
Infirmary
Glove Factory
4ft. F.W.
O X F O R D S T R E E T
Hall
P.H.
Wes. Meth. Ch.
Chapel
Def.
S.P.
Cattle Pens
Drill Hall
P.H.
W.M.
N E W R O A D
Woodstock Union Workhouse
Goods Shed
S.P.
F.W.
F.W.
Smy.
Grammar School
F.W.
H I G H S T R E E T
Inn
Terminus
HENSINGTON WITHIN
School
Hensington House
Lodge
County Police Station
Almshouses
F.W.
Allotment Gardens
Smy.
F.W.
Hensington Gate
69
256
Hensington Lodge

Introduction

The presence of Woodstock Manor and later its successor Blenheim Palace have always been influential in the life of Woodstock. The use of the Manor by the early medieval monarchs, firstly for hunting and later as a place of residence, led to the development, if not the foundation, of New Woodstock where the kings retinue lodged and the trades necessary for their comfort and sustenance expanded. The importance of the older township of Old Woodstock diminished with the rise of its neighbour and the various charters granted to the later.

Despite some increases in trade with the building of Blenheim Palace, it is only in this century that the town has changed to any great degree. The centre of Woodstock is fairly compact and the houses here are generally old. Expansion has thus occurred around the outskits of this centre and in Old Woodstock to the northeast. A by- pass planned for the town was abandoned by the County Council and the roads remain busy with traffic. A desire o maintain the green belt has led to opposition to any further building of houses on the outskirts of Woodstock.

Due to its proximity to Blenehim Palace, Woodstock has become a major tourist attraction and many of the shops reflect this trade which plays an important part in the local economy. The Palace itself was not formally opened to the public until 1950 but certainly in the latter part of the last century events such as large gatherings of Liberal Party members and fire brigade competitions took place. The existence of a railway station was also influential to the towns development, but sadly the line was closed in 1954. Despite the influx of visitors that fill the town almost daily, there is still a sense of community here and a desire to preserve the past. This book preserves in pictorial form some of the changes that have taken place here within living memory.

SECTION ONE

Views Around Woodstock

A rather unusual Taunt card showing a stylised map of Woodstock Manor and its surrounding parkland, now Blenheim Palace. Woodstock Manor dates back to at least the 12th century and was used by early monarchs as a hunting lodge. Henry II reputedly kept his mistress Rosamund Clifford or Fair Rosamund nearby. Elizabeth I was imprisoned at Woodstock Manor by her sister Mary, but evidence suggests that even by this date decay had set in. After the Battle of Edgehill, Charles I stayed at Woodstock; the manor house was fortified and soldiers billeted in the town until the royalists surrendered to Parliament in 1644. Sometime around the building of Blenheim Palace, Woodstock Manor was demolished.

Market Place in Victorian Times. The ground floor of the Town Hall is open to facilitate the storage of the sheep and cattle hurdles for market day. There are no cobbles outside the Town Hall and the state of the roads leave something to be desired. On the right are the premises of Eldridges, ironmongers who also dealt in copper and brass whose shop was later used by two grocers and is now Vickers Hotel. The family retained possession of the premises until they were sold in the 1920s. It is interesting to note the distinctive porch canopy which dates from around 1800. To the left is Eccles printing office. The 1851 census shows William Eccles as head, who originated from Warwick. His son, also William was born in Woodstock around 1836 and was listed as a printer's apprentice and he succeded his father as printer, stationer and postmaster. On the far right, James Dean is mentioned in a 1869 Kelly's directory as an iron and brass founder and the Dean family traded as ironmongers from this site from the 1830s to about 1870. The building was later acquired by the gloving family Lay and that trade was carried on there for almost 100 years.

Park Street with Harrison's Lane on the right which was known as Frog Lane in medieval times and changed in the nineteenth century to Primrose Hill before it acquired its present name. The first building on the left is Garrett House, once a sweet shop. Just past it with the triangular sign is a guest house and further on the corner is a grocery and tea shop.

Looking south down Oxford Street, the building on the left is now the Punch Bowl, once the premises of the Grammar school which moved here when the original building next to the church was demolished and was also once used as a bank. Next to T.J. Horn & Sons, Cycle Agents is a small shop that was once owned by Miss Frith who made children's clothes and later by Mrs Peachy who ran it as a sweet shop.

High Street, Woodstock. One of the most interesting things in this photograph are the trees in the background behind the National School. These mark the site of Hensington House which was later demolished along with its gardens. The building with the people outside is now the Co-op and just by the lamp post is now the premises of Breckon and Breckon. Further to the right, this double fronted house is now a sweet shop and antiques shop. On the extreme right is Cromwell House.

High Street, Woodstock around 1910. On the left is Turill and Dew the grocers with a delivery wagon outside and Budd's the bakers handcart at the rear. On the right the Baptist church can be seen quite clearly and the house to its left was once the premises of Woodstock Social Club until it moved to Oxford Street. To the right of the chapel is No 11 High Street; this was the Prince of Wales inn (earlier the Jolly Farmers and the Dog and Duck). As the inn sign is missing this could indicate that the date is slightly later at 1915, the date the pub closed. The house in front of which the children are standing has been rebuilt.

Looking from the junction of Market Street and Oxford Street by the Kings Arms around the turn of the century. The imposing building on the left is the Marlborough Arms. It is interesting to note the gas lamp in the centre of the picture, gas lighting being introduced to Woodstock around the middle of the nineteenth century.

This Taunt photograph of Market Street in 1905 shows the premises of Thorpe the chemist on the left and further down the Blandford Arms. This public house had closed for a few years in the middle of the last century and had been reopened by Morlands Brewery in 1869; beyond this is the premises of Maiseys the plumbers and Bartholemew House.

The Town Hall, probably in the 1890s. There is a poster for the Athletic Club in the left hand arch and the ground floor is open. To the left the large tree can be seen at the end of Market Street and to the right the premises of William Jardine, grocer and provision dealer.

Oxford Street looking south. On the extreme left is the Adam and Eve pub, with its sign in place. Two doors up from Smith's stores is Fox House occupied as an antiques shop. Past the Marlborough Arms is the Roof Tree, On the right next to the electricity pylon is Strong and Morris, then Pitts the fishmongers and Longworth's garage.

Oxford Street looking north around the turn of the century. The large tree in the centre of the town was presumably felled to improve the road which can be seen as a dusty track; when this happened is not known. Behind the tree these premises were once occupied by Atherton and Clothier, the gloving firm.

A similar view taken a little further south indicates that within a few years of the above photograph the tree was felled. On the right with the group of people outside is Hope House.

The Bear Hotel in 1906, when as the card tells us, H. Hawkins was the proprietor. The Bear acquired the block with the carriage entrance when it merged with the King's Arms, one of the local pubs that changed premises on occasions. The Bear expanded by absorbing buildings from either side during this century.

Probably taken about the same period, although there is a car! Just to the right of the tree is Garrets House.

Chaucers House outside the Woodstock Gate entrance to Blenheim Palace. When the courtyard was built in 1723 a house that extended from Chaucer's House to the park was demolished.

Looking south towards Woodstock from the fields behind Manor Farm, the date is probably the 1890s. The rear of the Olivet chapel can be seen to the left of centre and it is easy to follow the path of the road to north and south. However, it has proved impossible to give a definitive opinion as to the identity of the buildings on the extreme left. It is likely that to the right of the white house is Union Street and to the left possibly the fever hospital.

Taken some years apart, these two photographs of this row of cottages in Banbury Road show the changes of a tiled instead of thatched roof and the addition of drainpipes. These cottages were originally a row of five and have now been converted into two. Evidently not all the thatch was succesfully removed, some being found in the roof space at a later date.

Taken around 1928 this aerial photograph shows how much Woodstock has changed. To the left the modern houses in Lower Brook Hill are yet to be built whilst on the right the Woodstock Union Workhouse with its adjoining chapel can be seen.

E. N. HOARE

General Printer,

Stationer and Bookbinder,

Market Street, Woodstock

ALL COUNTRY ORDERS STRICTLY ATTENDED TO.

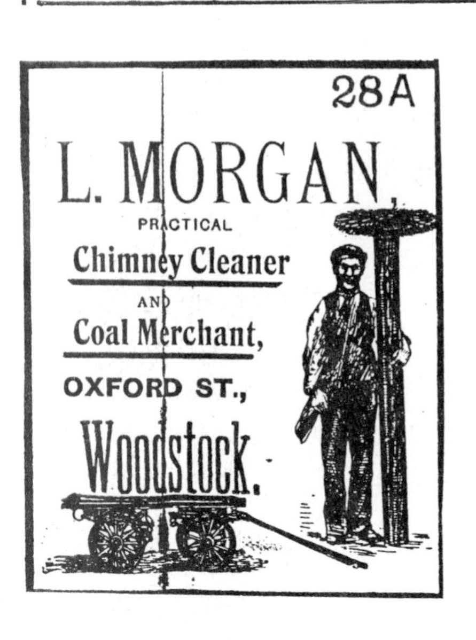

24

W. H. MAISEY, R.P.C.

Registered and Certificated by the Worshipful Company of Plumbers, London City Guilds.

. . *Sanitary Plumber.* . .

Gas, Hot-Water, and Electric Bell Fitter,

and House Decorator,

WOODSTOCK.

Houses inspected and their Sanitary condition reported upon.

Agent for the Climax Safety Valves and Welsbach Incandescent Gas Light Co's.

EXCELLENT TESTIMONIALS.

11 Years Practical experience with Mr. George Jennings, Sanitary Engineer, Lambeth, London.

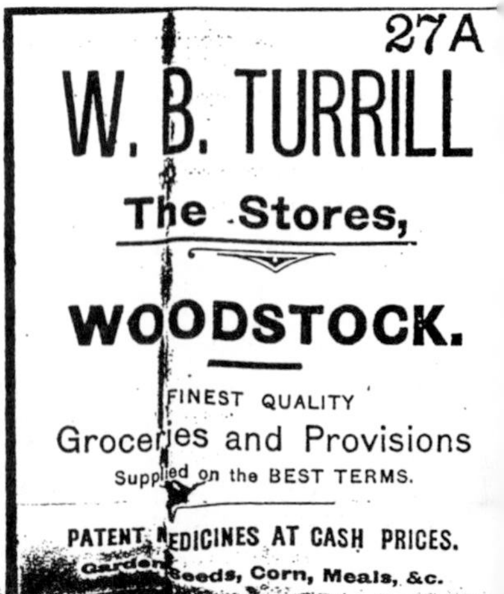

SECTION TWO

Employment

Banbury's clothing stores. From left to right: Gabriel George Banbury, John Banbury (Captain). In the upstairs window to the right of the London House sign a woman and two more children can be seen.

The shutters drawn in Banbury's windows and decorations put up for some special occasion. As the Stars and Stripes can be seen, it is likely that it is 1896 and the occasion the arrival of the 9th Duke of Marlborough and his American bride Consuelo Vanderbilt.

William Poore Clarke was an ironmonger with a shop in the Market Place in the later part of the last century. Certainly he was mentioned in Kelly's directory in 1883-1899 and in 1887 was also mentioned as an insurance agent and a agricultural implement agent. He was an alderman in 1886 and in 1899-1901. This card was posted in 1908. In the middle of the seventeenth century the house was the Three Cups inn.

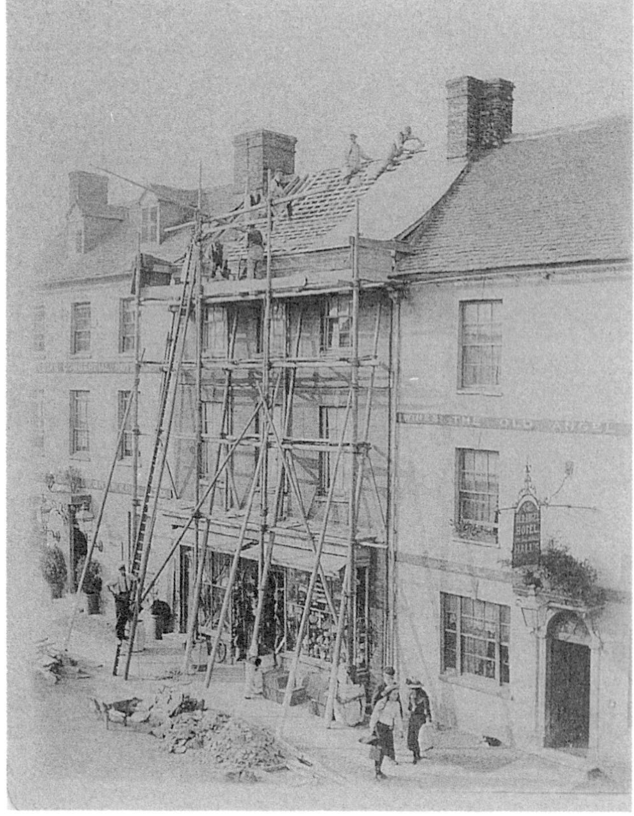

This is an unusual shot showing the scaffolding that was used in this period. To the right is the Old Angel, later the National Provincial Bank and also the site of the Angel Yard used on market days.

Presumably taken at an agricultural show or its equivalent, the card with the machines was posted 14 July 1909.

Dairymaids for the Duke of Marlborough taken at the cowyards off Woodstock Road. Left to right: ?, ?, Christine Brooks, ?, Phyllis Berry, Sybil Webley, Hilda Knibbs, Gretchen Brooks.

Photographed outside the Bear Hotel around 1920, C.W. Banbury at the sheep market which ceased just over a decade later. Various fairs were held in the town over the years and were noted for different commodities such as cheese and horses. By the late 19th century when 'a 1000 sheep were regularly sold,' the sheep market was held outside the Town Hall.

Sergeant Edward Jordon in uniform. He was a Londoner who fought at Ypres and Mons serving as a policeman both before and after World War I. He also worked at Scarsbrook's the timber Merchants after his retirement from the police force.

OXFORDSHIRE CONSTABULARY

Certificate of Conduct

This is to Certify that *Edward Jordon* a native of *Stoke Newington* in the County of *London* joined the Oxfordshire Constabulary as a *Constable* on the *twenty-seventh* day of *May 1912. and was pensioned on completion of service* when holding the rank of *Sergeant* on *27th. May 1937.* during which period his conduct was :— *exemplary*

Description of the above-named *Edward Jordon*

Age *49 years* Hair *dk brown*

Height *5 ft 11 ins* Complexion *fresh*

Eyes *hazel* Marks *Tattooed both arms*

This Certificate is without erasure of any kind.

E.K. [signature]

Chief Constable of Oxfordshire.

Doctor Frank Bevan came to Woodstock in 1932; during World War 2 he was a major in the Royal Army Medical Corps.

Doctor Henry Tothill was Dr. Bevan's partner and managed the practice with the help of locums during the war years.

This was the first tractor that Scarsbrooks the Timber Merchants owned and dates from about 1930. Left to right standing: Arthur Scarsbrook, Fred Scarsbrook. On the tree Jack Scarsbrook, Walter Freeman, Frank Lewington.

This was the last tractor owned by the firm which sadly closed in 1972.

The largest cedar tree in Britain was felled by Scarsbrooks in Blenheim Gardens approximately 1946/47. An Avon power saw with two 6 foot blades welded together to make one 12 foot blade was used for this job which took many hours. It was left overnight in High Street outside the radio shop for the public to see. It was then taken to the Scarsbrook premises where it stood at the bottom of the sawmill until 1972. On the left is Mr Castle of Tackley and on the right Mr W. Willis

Scarsbrook's workforce around 1945/46. Left to right back row: Jack Scarsbrook, Arthur Scarsbrook, Horace Bull, Sergeant Jordon, Jack Kennedy, Tom Robinson, Dick Hazell, William Britt (in the trilby hat) and Bill Shepherd (in the cap). Front row: Albert Berry, Titch Morris, Frederick Scarsbrook, Cynthia Scarsbrook, Aubrey Simmonds, ?, Fred Boyes, Ronald Slatter and Ron Bowler.

This picture was taken at the Coronation June 2 1952; the shop won the first prize for the window displays. Left to right: Joan Everard (nee Willis), June Fletcher (nee Willis, no relation), Sheila Pitts, Elsie Griffin (nee Pittick), Gwen Taylor (nee Willis), Iris Margetts (nee Pickett), Rosemary Giraud (nee Hine) and Whisky the cat. Smiths stores belonged to Joseph Burton and Sons of Nottingham. It was modernised about 1950 by Bowerman and Long.

During World War 2 the Ministry of Supplies was based at Blenheim Palace. Pictured here left to right: Miss Carson, Rosemary Hine, June Buckle (gardener at Cornbury Park), Betty Forbes, ?.

Woodstock Station around 1910. To the right of the track was the grounds of Hensington House and there was eventually a path linking the main road to New Road between the railway and the primary school next door. To the left of the track ran Hensington Road.

Mark Woolliscroft aged about 5 used to help pluck the Christmas pheasants and poultry at Pitts.

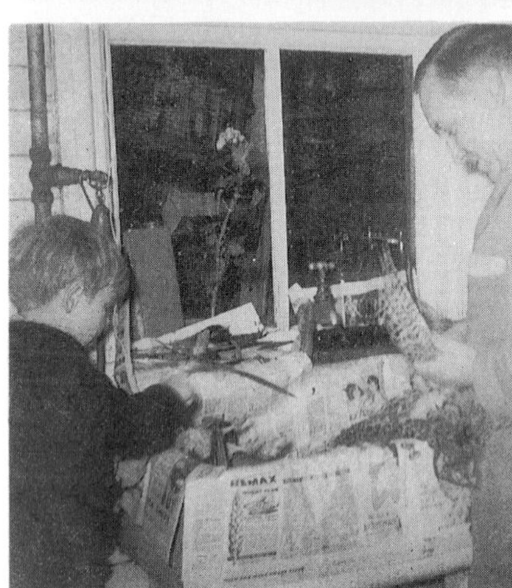

Mark is plucking a pigeon and Bill Pitts a pheasant.

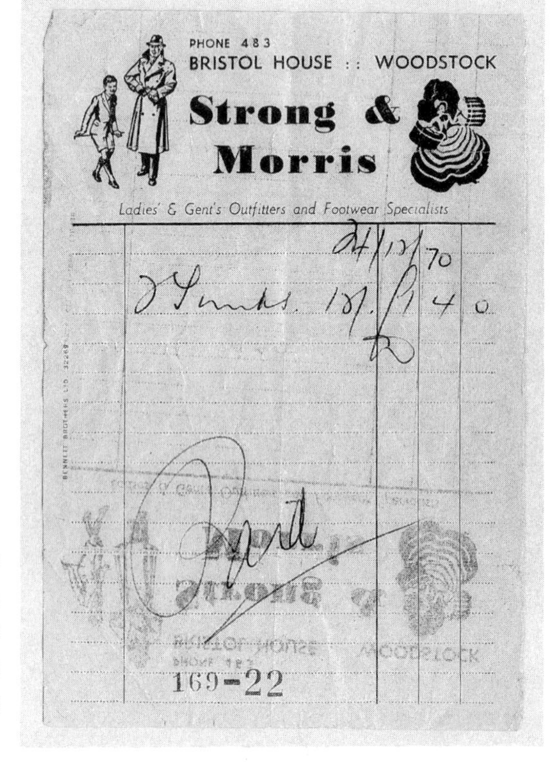

PHONE 483
BRISTOL HOUSE :: WOODSTOCK
Strong & Morris
Ladies' & Gent's Outfitters and Footwear Specialists

24/12/70

Paid

169-22

The origins of Strong & Morris can be traced back to the very late nineteenth century. The shop closed in 1980 and this billhead is a typical example of the type of receipt customers could expect before the advent of computers.

Robinsons butchers shop was situated in Market Street on the site later occupied by the Dorchester Hotel and later the Feathers. Tommy Robinson started a butchers shop in Woodstock in 1898 in Oxford Street and then became the landlord of the Blandford Arms. He opened the butchers shop on these premises and a dairy on the other side. He had a milk round in Hensington and Old Woodstock as well as the town; the cart was drawn by his pony Toby who regularly received a sugar lump from Mrs Stroud in Old Woodstock. Outside the dairy was a tree which Toby could be tied to. When Tommy Robinson retired in 1947 his son Harry took over the butcher's shop and his other son Tom took over the farm at Middle Barton. The shop closed in 1965 when Harry retired to Begbroke.

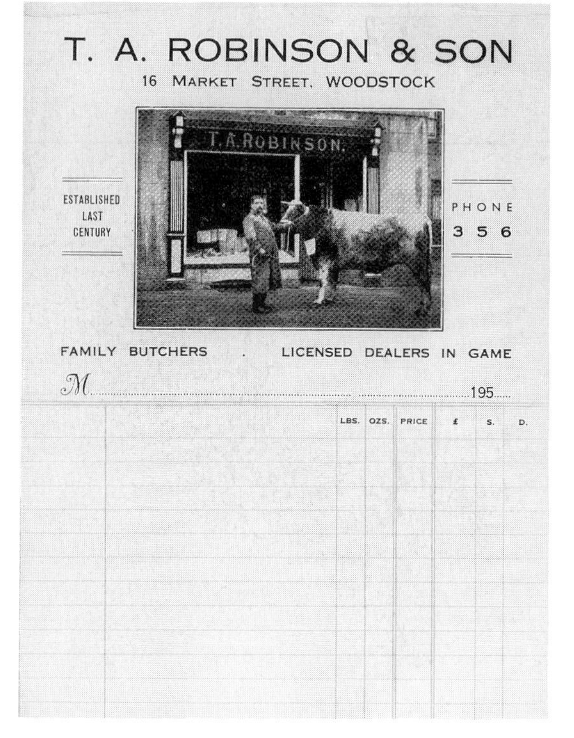
T. A. ROBINSON & SON
16 MARKET STREET, WOODSTOCK

ESTABLISHED LAST CENTURY

PHONE 356

FAMILY BUTCHERS . LICENSED DEALERS IN GAME

M .... 195.....

	LBS.	OZS.	PRICE	£	S.	D.

Robinsons Bill head

Tommy Robinson in his shop with a piece of beef. This photograph was taken by a Canadian photographer of a typical English butcher and published in Canada. The original was sent to Tommy Robinson.

Mr and Mrs Robinson outside Rothsay House after his retirement in 1947. Tommy Robinson was born in 1871 in Chipping Norton. At the age of 16 he was managing a butcher's shop in Great Leicester Street in Birmingham. He later had his own shop in Vauxhall Road, Birmingham. He was elected as a member of the Town Council in 1935, regularly topping the poll until he retired in 1946. He was a wonderful raconteur with a wealth of racy stories which kept his audience enthralled. He died on 15th January 1950, his wife dying the previous year.

Sidney Taylor was born in Woodstock but went to Sussex as there were few openings in the grocery trade. In 1932 he took over Number 7 Market Place, first renting and then buying the premises when the leasehold became vacant and running a grocery and provision shop. Both of the Taylor children were born here, in the room above the left hand shop window. The family lived here until Mr Taylor retired in 1965.

One of the previous occupants of these premises was 'Tinker' Eldridge, a bachelor who ran an ironmongers. Reputedly he was well off but when he died no money was found. The Taylor children had great fun tapping on walls to see if they could find any treasure. A well in the garden that had been covered in for safety reasons when the children arrived was suggested as a possible hiding place; however nothing was ever found.

Mr Taylor carried out some alterations, the rendered facade was removed to reveal its original stone and the windows were slightly altered.

Produce displayed outside Taylors shop.

Sidney Taylor with his wife Cecilia and daughter Jill at the rear of number 7.

A passageway led through to the rear of the shop and some of the shops provisions were stored at the bottom.

Bernice Osborne photographed in Lance Clothiers shop in Market Place. Although she normally worked in the shop, at busy periods Mrs Osborne helped out with some of the various stages of gloving. Seated at her machine she is stitching the welts.

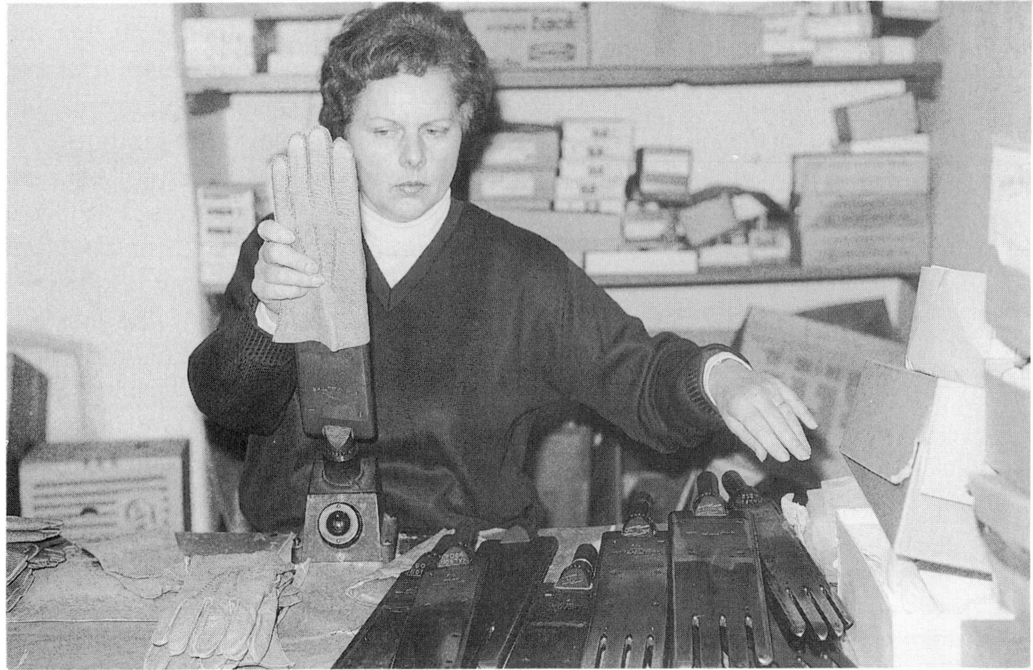

This machine pressed the gloves, after they had been put on the hot 'hands', they were smoothed down for a set time.

Presentation of safe driving awards about 1951 to drivers at the cement works at Shipton on Cherwell, most of these drivers are from Woodstock. Left to right back row: Lou Labracane, Jim Franklin, ? Hickson, Tec Heritage, ?, Jock Simpson, Phil Moss, Ken Smith, ? Thorpe, Eric Symons, George Merry. Front row: John Lewington, Charlie Peachy, Les Search, Bert Howes, Charlie Fozard, Mr Jupp (Works Manager), Mick Woodley, Tom Ward, Fred Blackwell (later Mayor of Banbury twice), Willie Watson, Harry Painter.

Ann and Dulcie Smith took over No. 30 High Street from Mrs Rendle on 23 September 1974 and continued to run it as a sweet shop. Previous proprietors of these premises have been Brian Knowles (Brian's), Mrs Timms, Mr and Mrs Jones and Mrs Hickman. Ann and Dulcie always wear matching clothes which has become quite a gimmick. The shop window has received six first prizes in the best dressed window section of Woodstock Carnival and at times such as Christmas and Halloween children especially enjoy the displays. Dulcie, Ann and her daughter Sarah also participate in the carnival itself raising money for the Cardiac Unit at the John Radcliffe Hospital. Taken outside their shop, this photograph shows their trademark: show the legs! The family has been involved in other businesses in Woodstock over the years: saddlers, coal merchants, timber merchants, TV and radio shop and DIY (J & S Supplies).

SECTION THREE

Church and School

Taken around the turn of the century this photograph of John Banbury with a group of young ladies is probably a Methodist Sunday School group. The photograph was taken at the rear of London House.

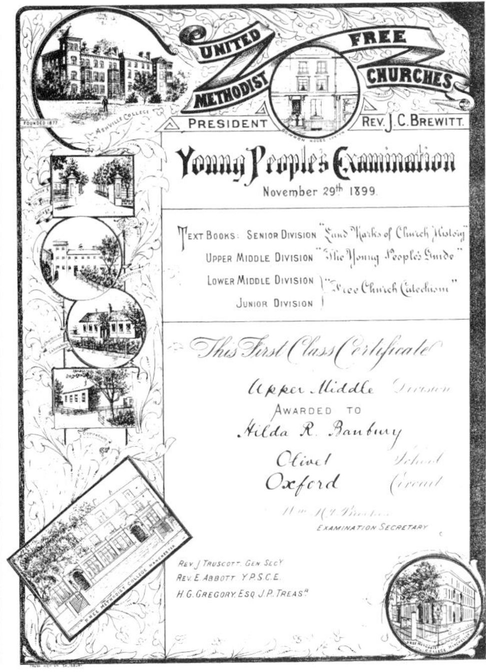

UNITED METHODIST FREE CHURCHES

PRESIDENT REV. J. C. BREWITT.

Young People's Examination

November 29th 1899.

TEXT BOOKS: SENIOR DIVISION "Land Marks of Church History"

UPPER MIDDLE DIVISION "The Young People's Guide"

LOWER MIDDLE DIVISION / JUNIOR DIVISION "Free Church Catechism"

This First Class Certificate

Upper Middle Division

AWARDED TO

Hilda R. Banbury

Olivet School

Oxford Circuit

EXAMINATION SECRETARY

REV. J. TRUSCOTT. GEN. SEC.Y

REV. E. ABBOTT. Y.P.S.C.E.

H. G. GREGORY. ESQ. J.P. TREAS.R

Methodist certificate.

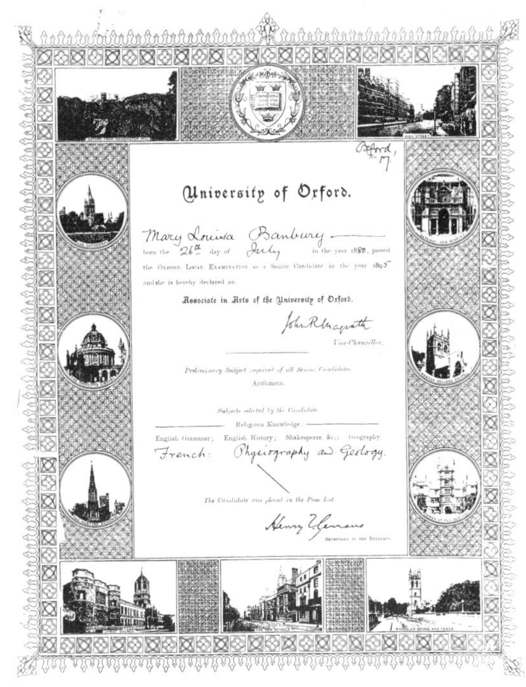

University of Oxford.

Mary Louisa Banbury born the 26th day of July in the year 1880, passed the Oxford Local Examination as a Senior Candidate in the year 1895 and she is hereby declared an

Associate in Arts of the University of Oxford.

Vice-Chancellor.

Preliminary Subject required of all Senior Candidates.

Arithmetic.

Subjects selected by the Candidate.

Religious Knowledge:

English Grammar; English History; Shakespeare &c.; Geography.

French: Physiography and Geology.

The Candidate was placed in the Pass List.

Secretary to the Delegacy.

University of Oxford certificate awarded to Mary Louisa Banbury in 1895.

Taken around 1920, this group of children attended Miss Baughan's private school.

A Sunday School outing, 1949/50 organised by Canon Pickles. Left to right back row: Ann Richards, Jill Danbury, Kathleen Holgate, Jill Taylor, Canon Pickles, Diane Holley and Margaret Smith. Front row: David Danbury, Roger Henman, Anthony Henman, ?.

Woodstock National School.

An aerial view of the old school in Oxford Road some time in the 1950s. The most striking thing about this photograph is the lack of traffic on the road.

Woodstock Primary School around 1930. Left to right back row: ?, Eric Buckingham, Doug Beckett, Roy Day, ? Freeman, Jack Scarsbrook, ?,?,Teddy Webb, Bob Townsend, Ron Scroggs. Second row: ? Styles, Cath Osborne, ?, Grace Grantham, ? White, Ivy Crutch, Iris Jordon, Nora Parsons, May Pittick, ? Morns. Third Row: Syd Jakeman, Jack Grantham, Joan Nunn, ?, ?, ?, Jean Pitts, Brenda Willis, Helen Prior, Reg Cooper. Front row: Jack Dempsey, Robert Mitchell, Jack Guy, Archyman, Norman Jerrams, Harry Freeman.

Mrs Dykes class around 1937/38. Left to right back row: Rosemary Hine, Esme Danbury, Cynthia Hollis, Margery Ruttle, John Axtel, Ray Philips. Middle row: Violet Hookway. Ann Durstan, Sheila Heath, Beryl Faulkes, Raymond Dicks. Front row: Terence Alkerton, Brian Lewington, Leonard Buckingham, Frank Brooks, Douglas Turner.

Woodstock Primary School, July 1959. Left to right back row: Brian Miller, John Simmonds, ? Fry, Derek Beckett, ?, Nigel ?, ?, ?, ?, ?, Caroline Simms, Anna Taylor, Jane Steele, ?. Middle row: Valerie Knibbs, ?, Christine Turvey, Sue Herbert, Avril Taylor, Carol Hughes, Linda Jordon, Jane Hine, Carol Symons, Kenta Eagle. Front row: Darrell Conway, ?, ?, Malcolm Holley, Leslie Knight, ?.

A Marlborough School group, November 1946. Left to right back row: Maureen Wickson, Betty Walton, Enid Willis, Daphne Hunt, Gwen Reed, Margaret Dix. Middle row: Barbara Mills, Jean Berry, Julia Howes, Sheila Pratley (from Long Hanborough), Beryl Aris. Front row: Daphne Cox, Janet Wastie, Jackie Howlett, Christine Smith, Bernice East.

Marlborough School girls about 1950. Left to right front row: Ann Leach, Pat Osborne, Ann Margetts. Second row: Maree Knibbs, Marguerite Rutherford, Marguerite Coleman, Betty Silvester. Third row: Betsy Adams, Tessa Badby, Miss K. Lea (Headmistress), Maureen Page, Iris Britt, Nellie Cadd. Back row: Megan Collins, Josephine Huckins.

A pottery class at the Marlborough School in the late 1960s. The girl at the back right is Ellen Appleby.

Some Marlborough girls in the 1960s. Left to right back row: Rachel or Melanie Adams, Michelle Symons, Teresa Cripps. At the front ?.

Marlborough School group. Left to right back row: Marylou Burden,?, Susan Brown, ?. Middle row: Peter Fordham, Mark Thomas, Elaine Pratley. Front row: ?, Theresa Cripps, Nicholas Appleby, ?, Kim Patterson.

The interior of St Mary Magdalene early this century.

The war memorial outside St Mary Magdalene.

Rev. Sherwood with H.R.H. Princess Margaret and His Grace the Duke of Marlborough attending St Mary Magdalene in the 1950s.

Bryden Alexander, draper, Market st
Bryden Mary Roden (Miss), draper, High street
Buckingham Charles, watch & clock maker, Market street
Budd James Gibbons & Son, bakers, High street
Caudwell Henry M.D.Durh.,L.R.C.P., L.R.C.S. & L.M.Edin. physician & surgeon, medical officer, factory surgeon & public vaccinator, Nos. 1 & 2 districts, Woodstock union, medical officer to the workhouse & assistant medical inspector of schools, Market street
Church House Club & Reading Rooms (George Budd, sec.), Park street
Clarke Wm. Poore,ironmgr.Market st
Clifford James C. tailor, Union st
CliftonJn.Plummer.blcksmth.Park la
Collett H. & Son, drapers, Market st. & glove manufacturers, Park street
Crutch William Hy. leather dresser, Old Woodstock
de Gruchy Wallace. confr. Market st
Dew John Herbt.pork butchr.High st
Eldridge Geo. ironmonger, High st
Fardon Druscilla (Mrs.), watch ma. High street
Farley Geo. & Son, builders, High st
Farrow Percy William. deputy supt. registrar of births, deaths & marriages, Park street
Franklin & Jones, auctionrs. High st
Gane Sidney, shopkpr.Old Woodstock
Gillett & Co. (Banbury Bank), bankers (Edward Sotham Davenport, manager), Park street; draw on Glyn, Mills, Currie & Co. London E C
Gouldrey Arth. hair drssr. High st
Green Abel, boot & shoe ma. High st
Greenwood Wilfred Sutcliffe, printer, High street
Guy Walter George, refreshment rooms, High street
Hall Henry, Star P.H. Market street
Hall Mary Ann (Mrs.), Angel inn, Market street
Hawkins & Higgs, solicitors, Park st
Hawkins Henry, Bear hotel, Park st
Haynes Charles & Son, plumbers & painters, Market street
Haynes William H. P. farmer, Manor farm, Old Woodstock
Henman Stanley, deputy registrar of births & deaths & registrar of marriages for Woodstock district & sec. Woodstock Charity Trustees, High street
Heynes Charles Bartholomew,builder, Old Woodstock
Higgs Arthur Gerald (firm, Hawkins & Higgs), solicitor, perpetual commissioner, clerk to county magistrates for South Wootton division, to the guardians & assessment committee of Woodstock union & to the Woodstock Rural District Council, registrar & high bailiff of Oxford county court, superintendent registrar of Woodstock district, steward to lord of the manor, His Grace the Duke of Marlborough K.G. clerk to commissioners of taxes & to Woodstock Sub-Committee of Oxfordshire Local Pension Committee, Park street
Holley Charles Frederick, insurance agent, Hensington lane
Hughes Thomas David M.R.C.V.S. Lond. & Edin. veterinary surgeon, & veterinary inspector under the "Diseases of Animals Acts," Oxford street
James Edward, Adam & Eve P.H. Oxford street
Keell Annie (Mrs.), stationer,Park st
Kent Israel, Prince of Wales P.H. High street
Kerwood Henry Thomas, farmer,Hensington farm
Knibbs Wm. J. carrier,Old Woodstck
Knott Maria (Mrs.),laundress,Park st
Lay Arth. Robt. glove manufr.Park st
Liberal Association (Mid-Oxon) (Adolphus Ballard, hon. sec.; F. A. Huckle, 10 Abbey rd. Oxford, registration agent)
Longworth Alfred, plumber,Oxford st
Longworth Emily (Mrs.), dress ma. Old Woodstock
Maisey Wm. H. plumber, Market st
Margetts Jn. whlwrght. Old Woodstck
Margetts Thomas E. Blandford Arms P.H. Market street
Matthews Edward, Woodstock Arms P.H. Market street
Matthews Edwin, saddler, Market st
Middle School for Boys (James H. Overton, master)
Mid-Oxon Gas Light & Coal Co. Ltd. (Edward Prescott, trustee),Park st
Mitchell James J. & Sons, builders, High street
Money H. K. & Sons, glove manufacturers, Oxford street
Morgan Lemuel, chimney sweeper, Oxford street
Morley Frederick, general smith, Hensington lane
Morris Alfred, cartage contractor, Oxford street
National Telephone Co. Ltd. (The) (N. F. T. Ward, mgr.), Oxford st
Newport Jane (Mrs.), shopkeeper, Old Woodstock
Osborne Geo. Crown P.H. High st
Paisley Wallace, travelling draper, Market place
Parker John, carpenter, Oxford st
Parker P. J. King's Arms P.H. Market street
Parker's Oxford Cycle & Motor Car Co. cycle manufacturers & dealers, Oxford street
Pentycross Alice (Mrs.), grocer, Old Woodstock
Pitts Fredk. fishmonger, Oxford st
Pratley Edwin, tailor, Hensington la
Pratt William Rowles, commission agent, Oxford street
Price John, restaurant, Park street
Price Victor Hy. boot ma. Oxford st
Pullman R. & J. Limited, glove manufacturers, Hensington lane
Purves George, boot dealer, High st
Radbourne Montague A. undertaker, High street
Raggett Sarah (Miss), dress maker, Oxford street
Roberts Neville, beer retlr. Oxford st
Robinson Thos.Albt.butchr.Oxford st
Rose Herbert, carpenter, High st
Russell John, Wheatsheaf inn, Old Woodstock
Salter Stephen, architect, High st
Sanders Misses, dress mas. High st
Sanders Geo. photographer, High st
Scarsbrook George & Son, saddlers, Oxford street
Shirley Chas. shopkpr.Old Woodstock
Smith George, Rose & Crown P.H. Old Woodstock
Smith Geo. Wm. grocer, Oxford st
Smith Henry, grocer, Oxford street
Snelgrove Edward J. inspector of police & billet master, Police statn
Spalding A. G. & Bros. glove manufacturers, Back lane
Steele Joshua, butcher, High street
Stockford Thurza (Mrs.), shopkeeper, Market street
Stone Ellen (Mrs.), tobaccnst.High st
Strong Chas.Alfd. boot ma.Oxford st
Sturgess Squad.-Sergt.-Major Chas. drill instructor B Squadron Oxfordshire (Queen's Own Oxfordshire Hussars) Yeomanry (Terr. Force), High street
Sykes Percival John, hair dresser, Market street
Taylor George Jn. builder, Oxford st
Taylor Wm.Hy.builder,Hensington la
Thorn Harry F. Marlborough Arms P.H. Oxford street
Thornton Herbert L.D.S.Eng.dentist, Market street
Thorpe Thomas Frederick, chemist, Market street
Turrill & Dew, grocers, High street
Voking George, King's Head P.H. Park lane
Ward George N. registrar of births, deaths & marriages & vaccination & relieving officer for Woodstock district, High street
Warmington John,cartage contractor, Park lane
Webley Albert, milliner, High street
Webley Alfd. Geo. glove mfr.High st
Whitlock Thos. butcher, Oxford st
Wiggins Frank, butcher, Oxford st
WilliamsThos.glove box ma.Oxford st
Willis Frederick Hy. grocer, High st
Willoughby William George, greengrocer,& borough surveyor & bailiff Woodstock county court, Market st
Woodstock Cemetery (Adolphus Ballard M.A., LL.B. clerk)
Woodstock United Permanent Benefit Friendly Society (J. F. Wickson, sec.), Oxford street

An entry from Kellys Directory c1910. (*Reed Information Services*)

SECTION FOUR

Civic Life

Woodstock Town Council on parade in the mid 50s. From left to right: Jack Painting (a special constable), F. Scarsbrook, Mr Long, Mr Ramsbotham, Dr Tothill, Charlie Denis (in the bowler hat), Fred Whitlock.

Left to right: Mr Sawyer the borough surveyor, Frederick Scarsbrook (councillor), Victor Tolley (Town Clerk).

Taken at a parade outside the Town Hall, 1941/42, Colonel Sir Eric St. Johnstone lived at Wessex Lodge and was in charge of the County police. On his left Leslie Wright M.M. who was a sergeant in the special constabulary.

The Red Cross in the 1950s. Left to right: Kath Smith, Mrs Jordon, Ann Bevan, Jess Henfrey, Rosemary Hine, Sylvia Dew, Betty Clifford, Miss Potter.

The Red Cross outside the Town Hall at a similar period. Left to right: Betty Clifford, Mrs Jordon, Rosemary Hine, Dorothy Lambourne, Margery Harper, Jessie Henfrey, Rosemary Henfrey, Pauline Tolley, Kath Smith, Nurse Newport, Nurse Bloomfield.

Woodstock Home Guard, Geoffrey East and Parley Bruton in the very early years of World War 2.

The officers of the Woodstock Home Guard company outside the Marlborough School, left to right back row: ? Launchbury, Victor Tolley, Geoff Green (from Stonesfield), Sidney Slay, ?, ?. Front row: ?, ?, Mr Sacre, Major Clowser, ? Bolsover, Michael Parsons, ?.

Woodstock Home Guard taken after D Day in 1944, left to right back row: ? Butler (manager of Co-op), Richard Ramsbottom, Harry Woodward (grocer), ? Wait or Wake. Front row: Audrey Turner (nee Wright), Alec Stuart, Major Clowser, Joe Arthur (quartermaster), Mrs Sinclair.

Inside Woodstock Town Hall around 1950, left to right Victor Tolley, Henry Tothill (Mayor), Cyril Morris, 10th Duke of Marlborough, Mrs Oliver, ?, Fred Whitlock.

Remembrance Sunday, 1967. Standard Bearer is Fred Johnson, Also included in this photograph are Mrs Tucker, Syd Jakeman, Tom Colyer, ? Wheeler, ? White, ? Green, Tom Robinson, Dennis Donovan, ? Robinson, Bill Parncutt, George Holley, Alan Corse.

Woodstock Town Council, taken Monday 23 May 1966 after the noon meeting. Left to right, back row: Mr J. Cameron, Mr F.W. Walker, Mr V.N. Tolley, Mr D.G. Williams, Miss J.M. Shelmardine, Dame Henrietta Barnett, Mrs J.M. Millar, A.A. England, J.N. Banbury. Front Row: Alderman C.W. Banbury, Mr Hollis (Mace Bearer), Mr M.E. Sawyer (Town Clerk), A.H.T. Robb Smith (Mayor), Mrs Robb Smith (Mayoress), Alderman C. Morris, Alderman E.H. Oliver, Alderman Dr H. Tothill. Council members not present: Mrs M.E. Bowley, Mr T. Hine, Dr. G.J.W. Snell.

Woodstock British Legion 1991. Left to right back row: Canon Beckwith, Les Hopkirk, Gordon Hollis, Doug Beckett, George Eustace, Peter Anderson (standard bearer), Frank Vickers, Gordon Woodward, Jim Dodd, Ron Jerrams, ?, ? Holiday, Kenneth Harse, Les Fitchett, ? Holiday, Vi Beckett, Ted Henderson, Wilf Pond, Major Cox, Mr Roncelle, Mr Appleton, Mr Miller, John Woolliscroft, Mr Onions, Gordon Mace, Owen Hughes, Bob Pickett, ?, ?. Front row: Maurice Gunton, Wyndham Vickers, John Daniels, Syd Jakeman, Leonard Rudman, Sid Smith, Ian Ramsey, Joan Ramsey, Mr Dickson.

The Royal British Legion, women's section in the early 1990s. Left to right back row: Betty Gunton, Jean Jakeman, Joyce Gibbard, Linda Pearce, Edna Pond, Hilda Hughes, Nicola Hollis, Maureen Bull, Freda Tracy. Middle row: Lily Scarsbrook, Hannah Britt, Pansy Fitchett, Nora Woodward, Daphne Dent, Jessie Rudman, Betty Revell, Mary Vickers, Sandra Price, Joyce Gott, Vi Waterhouse, Ellen Goodhall. Front row: Jean Hollis, Cicely Dodd, Anne Woodward.

The St. John's Ambulance team for the Woodstock area in the 1950s. Left to right back row: ?Tom Portlock, ?, ?,?, ?Keith Scroggs, Bob Warman, Frank Willis, A.J. Winch, ?, Bob Dixon. Front row: ?, Ruth Hoare (Nee Blackwell), ?, ?, ?, ?.

St John's ambulance on parade in Woodstock at a similar date. The leader is George Greening, Jim Winch, Bob Warman, Frank Willis, ?, ?, Tommy Thomson at the rear.

209

Details of Procedure, Poppy Day 1928

Poppies &c ordered.

3d Poppies 1500. Chaplet of Green Cycus leaves & Poppies
6d " 800 (33" x 22") for British Legions tribute
1/- " 200 for War Memorial 25/-
1d " (Childrens, not ordered but included with others). 1 Large Poster. 50 Small Posters
12 Giant Poppies for use on cars. 250 25 Window Bills. 10 Motor Car Bills
50 Sellers badges. Labels for Collecting boxes. 100.
Collecting boxes. 12. 25 Trays. 50 Side Clips for boxes
Discs for do 88.
Also another ½ dozen 2/6 Poppies

Poppies, &c issued.

Woodstock &c (Miss Read)

3d Poppies	300	20 Collecting Boxes
6d "	200	20 Poppy Trays
1/- "	100	40 Sellers Badges.
2/6 "	12	

Bills & Posters issued to

E. Hall (Woodstock) J. Baines
Mrs Evetts, Tackley A. E. Banbury
Miss Mansell Church Hanboro C. Morris
R. Pitts
– Ainge (Kid.
F. Judd (Wootton
J. Witts.
E. Bedford

Handborough (Miss Mansell, Church Hanborough)

3d Poppies	= 200	3 Each of Trays
6d "	= 120	Collecting Boxes
1/- "	= 12	Sellers Badges.

Tackley Mrs Evetts

3d	= 150	2 Boxes
6d	= ~~100~~	Trays
1/-	= 12	Badges.

Kiddington (Mrs Gaskell)

3d Poppies	= 75	2 Each Trays
6d "	= 50	Collecting Boxes
1/- "	= 10	& Sellers Badges.

Coombe (Rev. A.H. Pearson)

3d	– 120	3 Trays
6d	– 75	Boxes
1/-	– 15	Badges.

Glympton (Mrs Barnet) Wootton (Miss Judd) Stonesfield (Miss Gardner) Begbroke (Rev A H Gillmor)
3d Poppies 2 Each 3d = 150 2 Each 3d = 120 3d = ~~100~~ 125

Entry from British Legion 'Poppy day' collection records.

SECTION FIVE

Recreation

Ernest Banbury in the garden of London House around 1902. He had served in South Africa during the Boer War. The cup is inscribed 'Presented to Sergeant E. Banbury as a momento of the services he rendered to his county with the Imperial Yeomanry Hospital in South Africa Woodstock 1901'.

Gabriel George Banbury and family, including Ernest.

Bill and Norman Banbury in the garden of London House looking towards Union Street.

Left to right Millie Whillan, Mrs E. Banbury, Ernest Banbury and at the front Tom Whillan.

Josiah Hine outside his house decorated for some celebration, possibly something connected with the Marlborough family or even the relief of Mafeking; he was private secretary to 3 Dukes. This house is Nos 28-30 High Street, now the premises of Dulcies sweet shop and Bees Antiques.

Pictured here are Joseph Margetts with his wife Sue and sons Fred, George and Arthur and daughter Milly (later Judd). Joseph was the son of John Margetts, a glover and it is probable that he too followed this trade.

A rather unusual setting for a family group outside the Hensington Gate entrance to Blenheim Palace in 1906. The building on the right of the picture is the National School. Left to right back row: Rosa Bruton, Charles Bruton. Front row: Frank Bruton, Janet Bruton and Charles Bruton. The little girl at the front is Agnes Bruton later East. The family lived in Old Woodstock for the first years of Agnes' life.

By the mid 1920s the Bruton family were living at Number 5 Union Street. Left to right back row: Parley, Rosa, Charles, Agnes and Frank; at the front their parents Charles and Janet.

Agnes and Geoffrey East with their daughter Bernice outside their home in Union Street.

Bernice East with her grandmother Janet Bruton about 1933 at Number 2 New Road (now Number 4). The hedge behind them separates Number 2 and Number 4.

Tommy Robinson and his wife Maria nee Murphy outside Begbroke Priory.

Taken in 1937 in the garden's of Bartholomew House, the home of the Farndons. Left to right back row: Harry Robinson (took over the butcher's shop after his father), Vi Robinson, Tom Robinson (did the milk round). Front row: Maria Robinson (nee Murphy) and Tommy Robinson.

Outside the National Provincial Bank, now the National Westminster on the occasion of the proclamation of King Edward VII, 23 January, 1936. The lady in the middle of the front row with the clasped hands is Cis Freeman and to the left looking over her shoulder is Jess Payne. Mrs Lily Scarsbrook is on the far right with her daughter Ann.

Memorial service parade to the late King George V, January 28 1936. The boy at the front wearing gloves is Stan Peake, the lady in the middle in a fur coat is Mrs Annie Willis, to her right is Win Clack and behind her Flo Clack. Other ladies identified in this photo are Mrs Dobbin and Mrs Taylor.

Coronation Day outside Taylor's grocery shop before the rendered front was removed. The tall gentleman at the middle back is Sidney Taylor, and running right to left from him are Mr Gardner, Charles Taylor, Hilda Gardner (nee Taylor), Mont Pickett and Cecilia Taylor. Sitting in front of Mont is his wife Norah and on her lap is Dennis Taylor. (*OPA*)

The coronation day celebrations for George VI, May 12 1937. Unfortunately none of these children have been identified. (*OPA*)

Coronation Day 12th May 1937, looking from the Town hall up Park Street. The large flag at the front helps to hide the electricity pylon. Woodstock Town Council outside the Town Hall, presumably earlier in the day.

More Coronation Day celebrations, a childeren's fancy dress parade in High Street. Both of these pictures are produced from early colour photographs which have become very faded.

Taken at Mount Pleasant in Harrison's Lane, Alice Jane Wright with her son Henry Butler Wright, his daughter June De'ath and her baby Martin De'ath. The date of this photograph is 1942, the year Alice died.

Park Lane about 1956, possibly in the spring or autumn as the children are dressed for different seasons. From left to right: Susan Painting, Dulcie Smith, Alan Roberts, Christine Palmer, Angela Scarrott, Gillian Palmer.

Woodstock Football Charity Cup. Left to right: William Taylor, Grace Malin, Frederick Scarsbrook.

Woodstock Town Football Club 1st Eleven, October 1956, the winners of the Senior League Cup and the Charity Cup. Left to right back row: John Osborne, Brian Faulkes, Donald Osborne, Jimmy Hunt, Ray Hagar, Gil Ingham, Johnny Couling, Alec Morton. Front row: Ivor Gubbins, Stan Peake, Reg Hawkins, Jimmy Doherty, George Sulik.

Woodstock Harriers in the late 1920s. Left to right front row: Mr Scroggs (in suit), ?, ?, Ralph Taylor (holding the cup), Doug Miles, ?, Bob Peake, ?, ?, ?. Middle row: (in white) Albert Holloway, ?, ?, George Peake, ? Morley, ?, ?, (Ginger) Duffield, ?, Eddie Bradley, ?, ?. Back Row: ?, Bill Peake, ?, Harry Woodward, ?, ?, ?, Les Rose

Pegasus Football Club consisted of players from both Oxford and Cambridge. Two dedicated supporters are pictured here in the 1950s with their mascot, a peg! Left to right: Geoffrey East and Tommy Silman.

Woodstock British Legion in 1924, the winners of the Tug of War challenge. Left to right back row: ?, Alf Godfrey, Jim Stroud, ?, Les Wright, Edward Jordon.

The Scarsbrook float at George V Silver Jubilee celebrations in 1935. The building on the right is the Union Workhouse, now demolished and replaced by the fire station, library and police station. The cottage on the left of the picture is not quite as visible now, a stone wall surrounding it .

The celebrations of George V Silver Jubilee, 1935. The lorry was driven by Jack Scarsbrook and the driver's passenger was Donald Taplin. Britannia is Ann Scarsbrook aged 5 and the first sailor is Cynthia Scarsbrook ages 15. Others identified are Lesley and Ann Mitchell, Marion Hall and Peter Baynes. This photograph was taken at the top of Union Street. The float was designed by Mrs A.L. Scarsbrook.

Charles Bruton on his allotment on Klondyke off Shipton Road in the late 1920s. This area has now been covered by housing and the Primary School, this photograph being taken approximately where the school now is.

Sidney and Cecilia Taylor at the sheepwash in Blenheim Park.

V.E. party for Hensington Without at the Marlborough School. Left to right, back row: Joyce Reed, Joyce Wilson, Rosemary Hine, Esme Gibbs, Lilian Savings. Middle row: Marion Hill, Phyllis Jones, Jean Bern, Josephine Berry, Julia Howes, Donald Manners, George Gibbs, Alan Littleton, Iris Gubbin, Betty Gubbin, Freddy Wilson. Front row: Reg Allen, Donald Jones, ?, ? Gubbins, John Profit, ? Savings, Brian Littleton, Gordon Adams, Patrick Howes, Frank Brooks.

V.E. party for younger children at held at the Marlborough School. Left to right back row: Shirley and Nancy Gubbins, Jean Knibbs, ? Gibbs, ?, ? Gibbs, Desmond Boyes, Judith Widicombe, Patrick Howes. Middle row: Freddie Gibbs, Ann Profit, ?, Ann Roberts, ?, Betty Gibbs, Kathleen Knibbs, Jennifer Manners. Front row: Gordon Hollis, ?, Terence Boyes, ? Moss, ? Dobbin, Ronald Gubbins, ?.

Hensington VE party, 1945. The house next to the cemetery in Hensington Road belonged to the Wickson family and the party was held in their garage due to inclement weather. Left to right front row: Anne Hollis, Brenda Dicks, David Danbury, Jill Danbury. Middle row: Johnny Degruchy, David Cooper, Brian Joy, Janet Joy, Shirley Clothier, Mary Longworth. Back row: Christopher Wickson, Ronnie?, Raymond Dicks, Keith Scroggs, Josephine Clothier, ?, Diane Bennett.

Taken in the severe winter of 1947, this photograph looks up Green Lane towards Hensington Road and the woodyard.

A cleared path in Market Place.

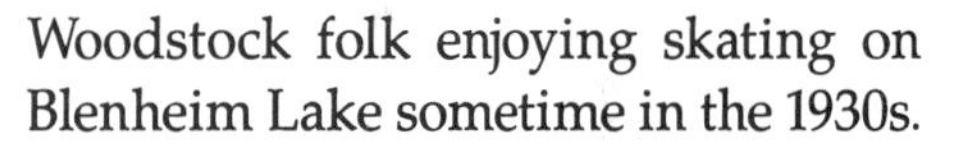

Woodstock folk enjoying skating on Blenheim Lake sometime in the 1930s.

Mrs Harriet Hine, Rosemary Hine, Thomas Hine and Mrs Mary Hine in the garden of their house in Shipton Road in the mid 1940s. It is interesting to note the railway embankment that runs along the back of the photograph.

Jane and Katherine Hine photographed at what is now the junction of New Road and Shipton Road in February 1956.

Haymaking in the 1940s where Churchill Close is now built: Lance, Josephine and Shirley Clothier. In the background is Dormer House.

Taken at a similar time, this photograph looks towards Wessex Lodge.

Looking from Hensington towards Bear Close in the 1940s.

A Youth Club outing. Left to right back row: John Whitlock, Eric Hudson, ?, ?, ?, Bob Dixon, ?, ?, ?, Reg Hawkins, ?, John Crosby. Middle row eighth from the left Louis Hunt. Front row fifth from the left Mrs Keynard and next to her Leslie Wood.

A Red Cross dance held at the Marlborough School, Oct 16 1953. Left to right back row: Mrs Hudson, Mrs Wickson, Mrs Barratt, Nurse Bloomfield, Fred Smith, ?, Miss Dew, Margery Harper, Miss Dodwell, ?. Front row: Betty Clifford, Pauline Tolley, Mrs Jordon, Mrs Potter, Rosemary Hine.

A meet outside the Bear, sometime in the 1950s. The hunt is almost certainly the Heythrop and the Duke and Duchess of Marlborough can be seen next to the central rider.

Singing carols around the tree traditionally placed in front of the Town Hall. The four people at the front of the photograph are Winston Morris, Pete Darrell and Octave and Rosemary Giraud.

At a social in the early 1950s. Left to right: Dorothy Britt, Mabel Griffin, Fred Griffin, Florence Griffin, Mrs Britt, Iris Britt.

Mark Woolliscroft and Hilary Coleman (Old Woodstock) on the galloping horses at Woodstock fair in the early 1950s.

Woodstock Pageant 1953 to celebrate the Quincentenary of the borough and the coronation of Queen Elizabeth II.

John and Marie Woolliscroft outside Ye Ancient House.

A King Charles II tableau. On the right is Marie Woolliscroft and next to her Mrs Morris.

Peter Page was chef to the Duke of Marlborough in the 1950s, he later became chef to H.M. Queen Elizabeth. He was a well known character in the town and now has retired in Windsor. Also on the left is Marie Woolliscroft.

A Hensington Without celebration in 1953 for the coronation. Photographed at a bar in the bike shed at the Marlborough school, left to right: Ron Scroggs, Percy Howes, Eric Symons, Albert Jerrams, George Knibbs.

Taken at the annual outing of the Woodstock Arms sometime in the 1950s. Left to right: Stan Hazel, Reg Hazel, Win Hazel, Margaret Gubbins, Topsy Symons. The coach is hired from Olivers in Long Hanborough.

Dennis Gosling was a well known tennis player in Woodstock. He is pictured here in the late 1950s with some local boys, probably at Bourton on the Water. Left to right: Paul Gosling, Rodney Woolliscroft, Mark Woolliscroft and Peter Gosling.

To raise money for Woodstock Swimming pool many events were held. This photograph of the Ladybirds float at a charity carnival in June 1972 taken outside the National Westminster Bank. From left to right on the float: Bernice Osborne, Betty Willis, Margaret Bishop and Mons Doherty.

Taken on the Barn Piece Estate left to right: Liz Hill, Terri Reynolds, Brenda Scroggs, Sue ?, Bernice Osborne, Betty Willis, Margaret Bishop, Mona Doherty, Sheila Dempsey (sitting on the float). By the float are Rose Collins and Martin Thorn.

Taken at the opening of the Woodstock swimming pool, Michelle and Louise Symons.

Before the swimming pool was built, mothers would take their children to the sheepwash in Blenheim. This was (and still is) an idyllic spot in summer where Woodstock children could play safely whilst their mothers could relax on the grass. Left to right: Beverly Symons, Carole Symons and Tricia Gubbins.

Woodstock Good Companions on holiday about 1960. Left to right back row: Kate Osborn, ?, ?. Front row: ?, Lill Charlwood, Florence Griffin, ?, Annie Horner.

The Queen's Own in the 1960s. Left to right: Archie Bradbury, Mrs Peake the landlady, Eric Symons.

Also in the Queen's Own at a similar time. Left to right: Baggie Perrin, ?,?, Ern Smith, David Peake, Eric Symons.

The old Social Club Christmas party in the 1950s. Left to right: Arthur Lewington, Marie Woolliscroft, Miss Webley and Bill Pitts.

At a social club football dinner, left to right Bill Pitts from the fishmongers and John Woolliscroft. It is interesting to note what is on the menu and compare it to what might be served today.

Taken at a football dinner at the old social club. Left to right: Harry Robinson, Vi Robinson, Marie Woolliscroft, John Woolliscroft, ?.

The new Woodstock Social Club was opened c 1977 around Christmas time. Left to right: Topsy Symons, Ann Ayres, Peggy Sulik, Shirley Townsend.

The first Woodstock charity carnival, sometime in the 1950s. The float entry depicted Big Bad Joe's Bar, Left to right: Mrs D. Stubbs, Marie Woolliscroft, Tony Marchant, R. Creber and Miss M. Wright.

Mrs Stubbs and Marie Woolliscroft at the carnival.

Woodstock carnival in the 1960s outside the grocery shop run by Taylors and then by Paynes, now a hotel. Left to right: Margaret Gubbins (lady with the dark cardigan over her arm), Carole Cooper, Kath Cooper, Topsy Symons. The children are Michelle and Louise Symons.

One of the floats at Woodstock carnival, left to right: Beverly Symons, ?, ?.

Alan England the compere talking to Beverly Symons.

Woodstock carnival 1968 outside the Town Hall.

SECTION SIX

Old Woodstock

Looking from The Causeway up the hill towards Old Woodstock. On the right is the Wheatsheaf and just to the left of the inn is Manor Farm. The water meadows are flooded.

Looking towards Woodstock from the Causeway, the pollarded willows can clearly be seen.

Looking from Hogrove Hill around the turn of the century over the roof of Whitlock's butchers shop towards Old Woodstock, this shop was later owned by Wicksons. Although the houses on the main road haven't changed the amount of traffic obviously has. At the top right is Barn Piece House and looking beyond is Barn Piece field, now a housing estate with Hill Rise in the distance.

A similar view but several decades later. The house at the bottom left was the bakerery owned by Barrets. Traffic is still minimal.

The Wheatsheaf public house around 1920.

Jack Russell was the landlord of the Wheatsheaf from World War I to 1934. Tom Ward then took it over until 12 July 1938 when he left and went to Bladon.

Rosa Willis with Frank around 1905, probably taken at 112/114/116 Manor Road.

These two ladies in Old Woodstock are Fanny Hawkins and her niece Edith Good.

Mr 'Shepherd' Kilbey and his wife. He worked for the Haynes family at Manor Farm in the early years of this century.

Mrs Martha Crutch and her daughter Nellie outside Turnpike Cottages around 1900.

Mrs Martha Crutch outside Turnpike Cottage Old Woodstock around 1910.

Alice Beckett, Sarah Emma (Cis) Crutch, Nellie Horn with Alice's daughter Annie Patricia about 1930.

Mr and Mrs Thomas Whitely outside the Glove House in the first years of this century.

Mr George Harper nicknamed 'Snotty' with his second wife in the 1940s. He was a coal merchant in Old Woodstock and had a yard on 'The Bank'. In later years he lived at 124 Manor Road.

Woodstock Mock Mayor in the 1950s. Left to right back row: J. Scroggs, W. Gardner, W. Perrin, W. Toogood, W. Warmington, E. Belcher, C. Webb, W. Payne, D. Long, A. Sharwood. Front row: G. Bowerman, Mrs Freeman, Mrs Holley, L. Stroud, F. Holley, Mrs Scroggs, Mrs Biswell, N. Freeman.

Around 1940, the corner of Barn Piece field, Old Woodstock looking north to Wootton. A housing estate has now been built here. Florence May Griffin with her niece Patricia Crutch (on the left) and a friend Sheila Launchbury.

Photographed on the hayrick in Barn Piece about 1950. Left to right: Violet Payne, Rosemary Henfrey, Eunice Barrett. At the back is Carole Morris.

Hill Rise at the same date. Left to right back row: Pat Crutch, Carol Morris, Frances Payne, Violet Payne. At the front Rosemary Henfrey, Jane Hine.

WOODSTOCK DIRECTORY. 815

Berry Geo. 29 New rd. Hensington Without
Berry Mrs. 64 Banbury rd. Hensington Without
Berry Mrs. W. 16 Hensington close
Berry Mrs. W. M. 29 High st
Berry Thos. A. 14 Churchill close
Berry Wm. 57 New rd
Besemer Mrs. C. A. Woodstock ho. Rectory la
Betts Ronald, 7 Hensington rd
Bevan Frank A., M.B., B.S. The Homestead, Grove rd
Bishop Margt. J. 15 Union st
Bishop Mrs. 5 Churchill close
Bishop Rt. J. 121 Manor rd. Old Woodstock
Biswell Jn. L. 30 Oxford st
Biswell Leonard, 77 Manor rd. Old Woodstock
Blakeley Gordon H. 117 Manor rd. Old Woodstock
Blowfield Leslie G. 1B, Rectory la
Bonasera Jn. 20 Churchill close
Bowen Wm. A. 15 Churchill close
Bowerman Alec, 5 New rd. Hensington Without
Bowerman Jas. F. 9 Manor rd. Old Woodstock
Bowerman Miss D. E. 64 Oxford st
Bowerman Rt. 8 Park st
Bowler Arth. W. S. 17 Park st
Bowles Mrs. E. F. The Retreat, Banbury rd. Hensington Without
Bowley Chas. C. S. 9 Oxford rd
Boyce Thos. W. 6 The Flats, Bear close
Boyce Wm. E. 40 High st
Boyes Desmond J. 31 Shipton rd. Hensington Without
Boyes Edwd. 1 The Flats, Bear close
Boyes Mrs. M. 68 Manor rd
Boyes Percvl. 39 Shipton rd
Brackenborough Mrs. C. 7 Bear close
Brading Brigadier N. B., C.M.G., O.B.E. 65 Oxford st
Bradley Edgar, 10 Park la
Braithwaite Jack, 27 Green la
Branchflower Jn. W. 19 Hill rise, Old Woodstock
Brett Donald, 125 Manor rd. Old Woodstock
Bricknell Graham, 53 New rd
Britt Mrs. H. E. 72 Manor rd. Old Woodstock
Brooks Benj. J. 7 Banbury rd
Brooks Chas. 27 New rd. Hensington Without
Brooks Edmnd. Jn. Long close, Oxford rd. Hensington Without
Brooks Geo. 82 Manor rd. Old Woodstock
Brooks Harry, 12 Market pl
Brooks Hy. 12 New rd. Hensington Without
Brooks Humphrey C. 3 Park st
Brooks Wm. 26 Bear close
Brooks Wm. 7 The Flats, Bear close
Brown Edwd. H. 26 Brook hill
Buckingham Mrs. 3 Bear close
Budd Mrs. 18 High st
Bull Hubert Jas. T. 4 Market st
Bull Sidney C. 13 Churchill close
Burden Jn. E. 111 Manor rd. Old Woodstock
Burke Mrs. M. 105 Manor rd. Old Woodstock
Burke Tom A. 105 Manor rd. Old Woodstock
Burton Fras. G. 7 Oxford rd
Butcher Geoffrey, 46 High st
Butler Herbt. W. 84 Oxford st
Bye Peter J. 16 Oxford st
Callander Jn. C. D. 24 High st
Cameron Jas. 14 Banbury rd. Hensington Without
Carter Alan, 7 Green la
Carter David I. 18 Park st
Castle Peter, 79 Oxford st
Castle Wm. K. F. 11 Market st
Cattell Fredk. H. 21 Green la
Chandler Stephen F. N. flat 1, 36 High st
Charlwood Alfd. 15 Hill rise, Old Woodstock
Chown Ronald T. 6 Green la
Clargo Edwin, 24 Cockpit close
Clay Miss E. A., M.A. 7 Park la
Clay Miss M. 22 Park st
Clews Ernest, 87 Manor rd. Old Woodstock
Clifford Anthony A. 3 Chaucer's la
Clifford Jas. 1 Bear close
Clifford Miss, 124 Manor rd. Old Woodstock
Clothier Lancelot, 18 Green la
Coates Ernest R. 2 Park st
Cockings Herbt. C. 13 Park st
Collier Geo. F. 25 Cockpit close
Collier Graham, 21 Bear close
Collins Mrs. E. L. 1 Union st
Conway Fredk. 42 Banbury rd. Hensington Without
Cook R. 64 Manor rd. Old Woodstock
Coombes Cyril L. P. 23 Bear close
Cooper Mrs. L. F. M. 15 Hensington close
Cooper Regnld. 110 Oxford st
Cooper Regnld. W. 23 Banbury rd. Hensington Without
Cooper Wltr. J. 70 Banbury rd. Hensington Without
Cox Mrs. G. N. 4 Park la
Cripps Terence I. 34 Green la
Cripps Wltr. J. 14 Hill rise, Old Woodstock
Croxford Miss V. D. P. 17 Shipton rd. Hensington Without
Crutch Albt. F. J. 26 New rd Hensington Without

An entry from Kellys directory 1964. (*Reed Information Services*)